POCKET

Diana

WISDOM

POCKET

Diana

WISDOM

Wise and Inspirational Words
from the People's Princess

Hardie Grant

BOOKS

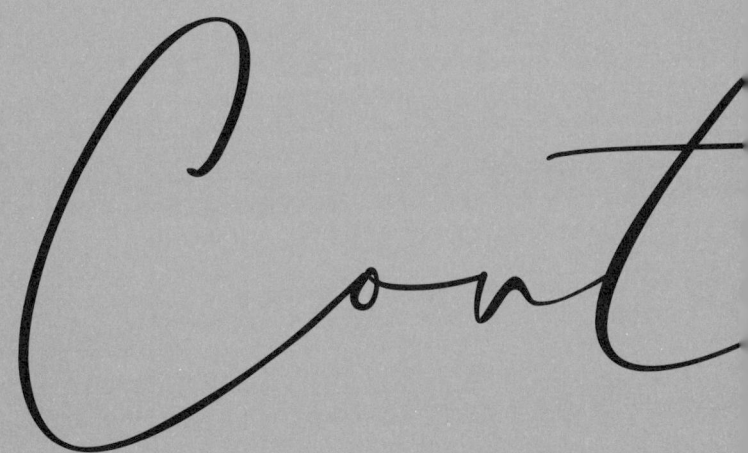

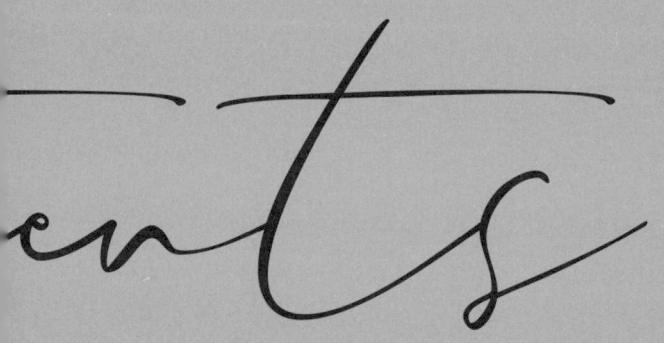

self

"I am a free spirit.
Some don't like that
but that's who I am."

"Maybe I was the first person to be
in this family who had depression,
or was ever openly tearful."

"What they say behind my back
is none of my business... But
I come back here and I know
when I turn my light off at night
I did my best."

"I wanted to get better to
continue my duty and my role as wife,
mother, princess of Wales."

"It took a long time to understand why people were so interested in me. I assumed it was because my husband had done a lot of wonderful work leading up to our marriage and our relationship...

But then... during the years
you see yourself as a good product
that sits on a shelf and sells well,
and people make a lot of
money out of you."

"I'd like to be a queen
in people's hearts."

"My first thoughts are that
I should not let people down,
that I should support them
and love them."

"Call me Diana,
not Princess Diana."

"I am not a political figure,
I am a humanitarian figure,
always was, always will be."

"I knew that something profound
was coming my way and I was just
treading water, waiting for it.
I didn't know what it was. I didn't know
where it was. I didn't know if it was
coming next year or next month.
But I knew I was different from
my friends in where I was going."

"The day I walked down the aisle
at St. Paul's Cathedral, I felt
that my personality was taken away
from me, and I was taken over
by the royal machine."

"Don't call me an icon.
I'm just a mother trying to help."

"I was unwell with post-natal
depression, which no one
ever discusses."

"I do things differently because
I don't go by a rule book, [and]
because I lead from the heart,
not the head. Albeit that's got me into
trouble in my work, I understand that.
But someone's got to go out there
and love people and show it."

"Anywhere I see suffering,
that is where I want to be,
doing what I can."

"I want to walk into a room –
be it a hospital for the dying
or a hospital for sick children –
and feel that I am needed.
I want to do, not just be."

"I knew what my job was;
it was to go out and meet people
and love them."

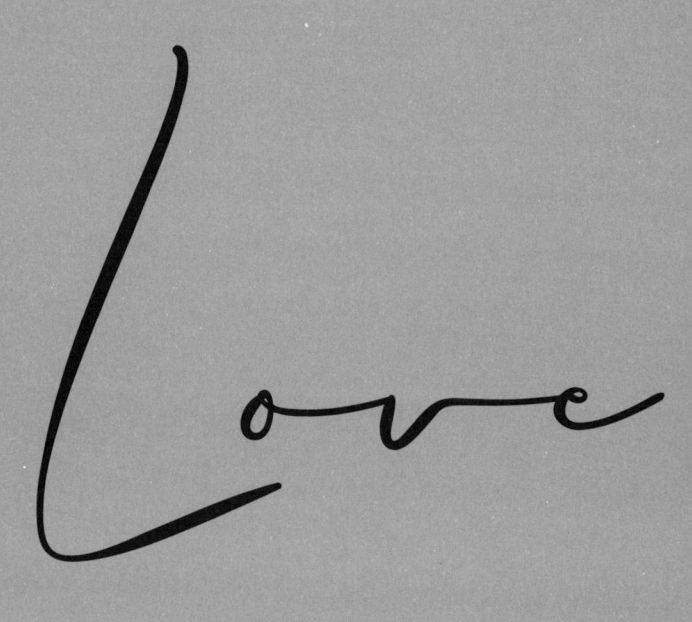

"I don't want expensive gifts;
I don't want to be bought.
I have everything I want.
I just want someone to be
there for me, to make me
feel safe and secure."

"The kindness and affection from the public have carried me through some of the most difficult periods, and always your love and affection have eased the journey."

"Hugs can do great amounts
of good – especially for children."

"I think the biggest disease
the world suffers from in this day
and age is the disease of people
feeling unloved."

"If you find someone you love in your life, then hang on to that love."

"Only do what
your heart tells you."

"If you were lucky enough
to find someone who loved you,
then you must protect it."

"I'm aware that people
I have loved and [sic] have died
and are in the spirit world
looking after me."

"I wear my heart
on my sleeve."

"I touch people.
I think everyone needs that.
Placing a hand on a friend's face
means making contact."

"Family is the most important
thing in the world."

"I want my boys to have an understanding of people's emotions, their insecurities, people's distress, and their hopes and dreams."

"I think like any marriage,
especially when you've
had divorced parents like myself,
you want to try even harder
to make it work."

"A mother's arms are more comforting than anyone else's."

"[Women are] On call twenty four
hours a day, seven days a week,
whether their children are sick,
their husbands are out of work or their
parents are old and frail and need
attending – they will cope...

They will cook and clean,
go out to work, attend to
the needs of those around them
– and they will cope."

"I will fight for my children
on any level so they can reach
their potential as human beings
and in their public duties."

"If men had to have babies,
they would only ever have
one each."

"Every young person deserves
a proper start in life, and those
who have no family to turn
to need to be able to rely on
us as a society for the help
and encouragement they need."

"As parents... we have an
obligation to care for our children
in ways that clearly show our children
that we value them. They in turn
will learn how to value themselves."

"The fairytale had come
to an end and my marriage
had taken a turn."

"Any sane person would have left long ago. But I cannot. I have my sons."

"I live for my sons.
I would be lost without them."

"What must it be like
for a little boy to read that
daddy never loved mummy?"

"William has brought us such
happiness and contentment,
and consequently, I can't wait
for masses more."

"Hugging has no harmful side effects.
If we all play our part in making
our children feel valued, the result
will be tremendous. There are potential
huggers in every household."

"I am only too aware of the temptation of avoiding harsh reality; not just for myself but for my own children too. Am I doing them a favour if I hide suffering and unpleasantness from them until the last possible minute?...

The last minutes which I choose
for them may be too late. I can only
face them with a choice based on what
I know. The rest is up to them."

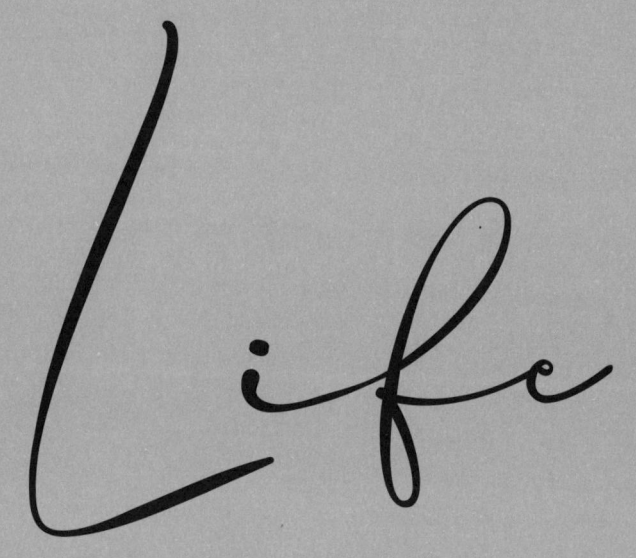

"Everyone of us needs to
show how much we care for
each other and, in the process,
care for ourselves."

"Carry out a random act
of kindness, with no expectation
of reward, safe in the knowledge
that one day someone might
do the same for you."

"I think every strong woman
in history has had to walk down a
similar path, and I think it's the strength
that causes the confusion and the fear...

Why is she strong? Where does she get it from? Where is she taking it? Where is she going to use it? Why do the public still support her?"

"Two things stand like stone:
kindness in another's trouble,
courage in your own."

"The greatest problem in
the world today is intolerance.
Everyone is so intolerant
of each other."

"When you are happy you can forgive a great deal."

"Putting a lid on powerful
feelings and emotions cannot
be the healthy option."

"Helping people in need
is a good and essential part
of my life, a kind of destiny."

"Life is just a journey."

"A woman's instinct
is a very good one."

"You can't comfort the
afflicted with [sic] afflicting
the comfortable."

"Everyone needs to be valued.
Everyone has the potential to
give something back."

"Perhaps, we're too embarrassed to change, too frightened of the consequences of showing that we care. But why not risk it anyway! Begin today!"

Cult

and

ure

Society

"They say it is better to be poor
and happy than rich and miserable,
but how about a compromise
like moderately rich and
just moody?"

"People think that, at the end
of the day, a man is the only answer.
Actually, a fulfilling job is better
for me."

"I have it on very good authority
that the quest for perfection in society
can leave the individual gasping
for breath at every turn."

"Let's not wait to be prompted, but let us go out tonight, tomorrow and the days that follow, and let us demonstrate our humanity."

"It's not sissy to
show your feeling [sic]."

"I remember saying to myself... 'You've been chosen to this position, so you must adapt to it and stop fighting it.' And I knew I could do it, if I chose a different angle."

"The beginning seems to be that women in our society are seen as the carers – the ones who can cope. Whatever life throws at them – they will always cope...

So deep seated is this belief
that it can take enormous courage for
women to admit they cannot cope."

"We, as a part of society,
must ensure that young people –
who are our future – are given
the chance they deserve."

"I love to hold people's hands
when I visit hospitals, even though
they are shocked because they haven't
experienced anything like it before,
but to me it is a normal thing to do."

"I think the British people need
someone in public life to give affection,
to make them feel important,
to support them, to give them light
in their dark tunnels...

I see it as a possibly unique role,
and yes, I've had difficulties, as everybody
has witnessed over the years, but let's now
use the knowledge I've gathered to help
other people in distress."

"Nothing gives me more happiness than to try to aid the most vulnerable of this society. Whoever is in distress who calls me, I will come running."

"We as a society owe it to women
to create a truly supportive environment
in which they too can grow and
move forward."

"When I started public life 12 years ago
I was aware that the media was
going to be interested in what I did,
but I was not aware of how overwhelming
that attention would become."

"Being a princess isn't all that it's cracked up to be."

Sources

Bashir, Martin. 1995. "BBC1 Panorama interview with the Princess of Wales." [Online] [Last Accessed 14.7.21] Available at: https://www.bbc.co.uk/news/special/politics97/diana/panorama.html – pp. 8, 9, 11, 12, 13, 14, 15, 16, 21, 22, 31, 32, 41, 42, 50, 62, 63, 68, 70, 77, 86, 87

Curry, Ann. 2004. "Princess Diana Tapes: Part 5". NBC.com [Online] [Last Accessed: 14.7.21] Available at: https://www.nbcnews.com/id/wbna6662336 – p. 18

Dampier, Phil. 2013. *Diana: I'm going to be me: The People's Princess Revealed in Her Words*, Barzipan Publishing – pp. 19, 20, 54, 85

Danielle Fowler, 2021. "13 Of Princess Diana's Most Inspiring Quotes." *Grazia Daily*, [Online] [Last Accessed: 27.7.21] Available at: https://graziadaily.co.uk/celebrity/news/princess-diana-quotes/ – p. 34

Diana, Princess of Wales. 16.1.1997. Angola: Luanda: Britain's Diana Princess of Wales Visit Update., Youtube.com [Online] [Last Accessed 14.7.21] Available at: https://www.youtube.com/watch?v=ibS0lVJ1f7M – p. 17

Diana, Princess of Wales. 2.12.1996. Centrepoint Speech, [Online] [Last Accessed: 15.7.21] Available at: http://www.aparchive.com/metadata/youtube/847e8aa339827d7fcf1170696dbe1f9f. – p. 48

Diana, Princess of Wales. 27.8.1997. Interview in Le Monde, 27 August 1997, [Online] [Last Accessed: 15.7.21] Available at: http://www.aparchive.com/metadata youtube/6ad55d1dd3aca6fdc7328e5c5f669103 -– p. 37

Diana, Princess of Wales, On Eating Disorders, 27.4.1993. [Online] [Last Accessed 14.7.21] Available at: https://awpc.cattcenter.iastate.edu/2017/03/09/on-eating-disorders-april-27-1993/– pp. 49, 78

Diana, Princess of Wales, Speech at the Headway Lunch, 3.12.1993. Peter Settelen [Online] [Last Accessed: 15.7.21] Available at: http://www.settelen.com/diana_mental_health.htm – pp. 29, 90

Diana, Princess of Wales, Speech given by Diana, Princess of Wales on "Women and Mental Health 1st June 1993, Peter Settelen.

SOURCES

[Online] [Last Accessed 14.7.21] Available at: http://www.settelen.com/diana_mental_health.htm – pp. 44, 45, 67, 82, 83, 89

Diana, Princess of Wales, SussexRoyal, Instagram.com, [Online] [Last Accessed: 15.7.21] Available at: https://www.instagram.com/p/B08vw-FF5Qa/?utm_source=ig_embed – p. 61

Diana, Princess of Wales. 1996. "Princess Diana in Washington DC, 1996". The Froth and Bubble Foundation for Food Assistance. [Online] [Last Accessed: 27.7.21] https://arizonanonprofits.org/news/471451/Froth-and-Bubble--Exactly-What-Life-Should-Be-Made-Of-.htm – p. 64

Diana, Princess of Wales. Does the Community Care?, 1993. Peter Settelen [Online] [Last Accessed: 15.7.21] Available at: https://www.settelen.com/diana_care_in_the_community.htm – pp. 60, 73

Diana, Princess of Wales. Princess Diana Speech on Addiction, 1989. Youtube.com [Online] [Last Accessed: 15.7.21] Available at: https://www.youtube.com/watch?v=CCWfDxFxNRg – p. 55

Diana, Princess of Wales. 7.12.1995. Speech on Homelessness. Youtube.com. [Online] [Last Accessed: 15.7.21] Available at: https://www.youtube.com/watch?v=TIMb6sTa2Uw – p. 84

Diana, Princess of Wales. 12.12.1995. The United Cerebral Palsy of New York. Youtube.com [Online] [Last Accessed: 15.7.21] Available at: https://www.youtube.com/watch?v=svCjAPnDUZo – p. 79

Diana, Princess of Wales. Women and Children with Aids, 8.9.1993. Peter Settelen [Online] [Last Accessed: 15.7.21] Available at: https://www.settelen.com/diana_women_and_children_with_aids.htm – pp. 56, 57

McDowell, Erin. 1.7.21. "13 times Princess Diana spoke candidly about her complicated life as a royal." Insider. [Online] [Last Accessed: 13.8.21] Available at: https://www.insider.com/princess-diana-quotes-about-her-life-as-a-royal-2020-6 – p. 81

SOURCES

Morton, Andrew. 11.8.2003 *Diana: Her True Story in Her Own Words*. Michael O'Mara, revised – pp. 10, 23, 36

Paprocki, Sherry Beck. 2009. Diana, Princess of Wales. Facts On File, Incorporated, page 62 – p. 43

Stedman, Emily. 30.7.2021. "Princess Diana quotes: 35 inspirational words on love, motherhood and life". Good to Know. [Online] [Last Accessed: 13.8.21] Last Accessed: https://www.goodto.com/royal-news/princess-diana-quotes 607184%20 %E2%80%93%20p.%2080 – pp. 80, 91

The Observer. 1984, July 29. [Online] Available at: https://www.historic-newspapers.co.uk/old-newspapers/observer/– p. 47

The Telegraph. 2018, June 2019. "Princess Diana's 15 most powerful and inspirational quotes", [Online] [Last Accessed: 27.7.21] Available at: https://www.telegraph.co.uk/women/life/princess-dianas-15-powerful-inspirational-quotes/do-heart-tells0/– pp. 33, 40, 72

Valemont, Pamela Lillian. 26.7.2012. *The Bible Code Princess Diana and Dodi Fayed*. Lulu. com.– pp. 24, 25, 30, 35, 46, 51, 52, 53, 65, 66, 69, 71, 76, 88

Voogt, Alan. 12.9.1997. *Princess Diana: The Book of Love*. Ten Speed Press, 11 – p. 28

Published in 2022 by Hardie Grant Books,
an imprint of Hardie Grant Publishing

Hardie Grant Books (London)
5th & 6th Floors
52–54 Southwark Street
London SE1 1UN

Hardie Grant Books (Melbourne)
Building 1, 658 Church Street
Richmond, Victoria 3121

hardiegrantbooks.com

Text © Hardie Grant

British Library Cataloguing-in-Publication Data. A catalogue
record for this book is available from the British Library.

Pocket Diana Wisdom
ISBN: 978-1-78488-495-6

10 9 8 7 6 5 4 3 2 1

Publisher: Kajal Mistry
Commissioning Editor: Kate Burkett
Editorial Assistant: Simran Kular
Design and Art Direction: Studio Noel
Production Controller: Sabeena Atchia

Colour reproduction by p2d
Printed and bound in China by Leo Paper Products Ltd.